What others are saying about Total Law of Attraction:

"Dr. David Che has actually accomplished a little miracle with his book, *Total Law of Attraction*. This is not just a book about the power of positive thinking, that anything is within our grasp if we truly believe and create it through our working with our subconscious: this is a book about changing the world in which we have been living into a place where gratitude, forgiveness, letting go of negative things and focusing on genuine happiness is entirely possible."

—Grady Harp, Hall of Fame Amazon Reviewer

"I've been a student of Law of Attraction for close to three decades . . . *Total Law of Attraction* is an amazing primer of basic stuff."

—Diana Page Jordan, Associated Press

"There is a lot of truth in this book. The book is very much 'step by step' and is easy to read. As a practical guide, I'd recommend this to anyone who wants to implement the Law of Attraction."

—Joanna Daneman, Amazon Top Ten Reviewer

"If you only read ONE book about the Law of Attraction, *Total Law of Attraction* will provide all you need to know."

—Alice Berger, *Bergers Book Reviews*

"I have always been fascinated by the ability of the mind to create one's reality and have read many books over the past twenty years about the topic. The author brings together the most powerful secrets on the Law of Attraction and explains it in a manner in which anyone can understand it. This is one of those rare books that I had trouble putting down and read it through in only a few sittings."

—Steve Burns, Amazon Top 500 Reviewer

"Plain, simple, and to the point, this book is the burger without the pickle relish, onions, mustard and ketchup—just the meat! I have been working with the Law of Attraction (LOA) for some time now. The instructions are all here, without having to read through pages and pages of filler. The goal here is to present the LOA in a fast and simple way, so the average Joe/Jane can understand it, practice it, and achieve success."

—Kathy W., Amazon Top 500 Reviewer

Total Law
of
Attraction
*Unleash Your
Secret Creative Power
to Get What You Want!*

DR. DAVID CHE

Gallery Books
New York London Toronto Sydney New Delhi

Gallery Books
A Division of Simon & Schuster, Inc.
1230 Avenue of the Americas
New York, NY 10020

Originally published in 2010 by Blue Note Books

First Gallery Books trade paperback edition October 2013

GALLERY BOOKS and colophon are registered trademarks of Simon & Schuster, Inc.

For information about special discounts for bulk purchases, please contact Simon & Schuster Special Sales at 1-866-506-1949 or business@simonandschuster.com.

The Simon & Schuster Speakers Bureau can bring authors to your live event. For more information or to book an event contact the Simon & Schuster Speakers Bureau at 1-866-248-3049 or visit our website at www.simonspeakers.com.

Interior design by Nancy Singer
Jacket design by James Perales
Cover photograph © Getty Images

Manufactured in the United States of America

10 9 8 7 6 5 4 3 2 1

ISBN 978-1-4767-5737-7
ISBN 978-1-4767-3369-2 (ebook)

Contents

Introduction   xi

Chapter 1
It All Starts with Your Beliefs   1

Chapter 2
The Law of Attraction and Quantum Physics   3

Chapter 3
The Conscious and Subconscious Minds:
What They Are and How They Work   9

Chapter 4
The ETHER in Space:
UNLIMITED Manifestation Energy   11

Chapter 5
How the Conscious and Subconscious Minds
Create Physical Reality Through the Ether   15

Chapter 6
The Not-So-Obvious Concepts
in Manifesting (Part 1)   17

Chapter 7

The Not-So-Obvious Concepts

in Manifesting (Part 2)   21

Chapter 8

Why BELIEVING Makes ALL the

Difference in the World!   23

Chapter 9

The Law of Detachment   27

Chapter 10

The Law of Detachment and the

Uncertainty Principle   31

Chapter 11

Express GRATITUDE for

Everything in Life!   35

Chapter 12

Being AWARE of Negative Possibilities

PREVENTS Them from Happening   39

Chapter 13

Never See the World the Same Way Again   43

Chapter 14

Taking ACTION at the Right Time   47

Chapter 15

Putting It All Together into a Practical Method

of Manifestation   51

Chapter 16

Some Things to Help Along with
the Manifestation Process 55

Chapter 17

Things That Are Very Difficult or
Impossible to Manifest 57

Chapter 18

Some Other Key Points to Keep in Mind 61

Chapter 19

In Conclusion 67

Bonus Chapter 20

A More Detailed Explanation of the
Law of Attraction and Quantum Physics 71

Bonus Chapter 21

Always Watch Your State of Emotions 75

This book is dedicated to the individuals who have been searching for the secrets of the law of attraction to dramatically improve their lives

Introduction

Read This First

The law of attraction and manifesting is talked about much these days. You've likely heard of the law of attraction, but what is manifesting? Manifesting is the act of bringing into physical reality what you think about. This book heavily emphasizes practicality and application over theory. Some basic theory is given in the chapters and is fully explained, but only when necessary to reinforce the practical concepts.

Many books out there give you a list of additional laws to complement the law of attraction, but no straightforward technique at the end to put it all together for you to APPLY to your daily life. Other books explain theory upon theory and never end up offering a practical method of manifesting. I know, because I have come across, studied, and absorbed much information from many of these books. I've searched and searched for a book that is able to make all the relevant theory and techniques easy to understand. If there is such a book, I haven't found it yet. I thought, "If it's not out there, then I might as well write one." I've talked to many people who say, "The law of attraction doesn't work," as well as similar comments.

The problem isn't that it doesn't work; it's just that it has never been presented in a simple way in which the average person can make practical daily use of it. Yes, the laws and theories pertaining to the law of attraction are somewhat complicated, but they can be greatly simplified into a workable manner for everyday use. It's like your cell phone. The science behind the inner electronic workings of your cell phone is complicated. But you don't need to know it to use the cell phone. Likewise, the law of attraction can be simplified so that it can be applied in daily life without the need to know the deep inner workings of it.

I have incorporated the other important laws into this book that work with the law of attraction, but I don't directly name them except for one, which you'll see later.

Many people think the law of attraction is something new. Actually, the law of attraction, like the law of gravity, has been around since the beginning of time. It doesn't command the respect and attention of the law of gravity because the effects of gravity can be seen and felt IMMEDIATELY—for example, seeing something fall from a great height. By contrast, the law of attraction almost always has a time delay and isn't so obvious. Most people can't accept the fact that something negative, which happened to them today is the result of a negative thought and emotion they may have had days or weeks before.

Please read this book in the order of the chapters. This is very important! Each chapter builds upon the information from the one before, and if you skip around, you will get confused.

All the information I'm revealing in this book is written in an easy-to-read, informal conversational format. It is very direct and straight to the point. I'm not holding anything back. Nothing is watered down and I won't throw you a curve.

Even though I designed this book to be as simplistic as possible, you'll STILL probably have to reread it a few times to fully absorb the concepts and make them second nature.

At times through the book, it will appear as if I am repeating myself over and over. I'm doing this on PURPOSE to drive home some very important points so you will fully understand the concepts.

I had a physics book in high school written by Lewis Epstein in which he said, "There's an easy way to explain anything; the HARD part is finding it." I believe I have achieved that in this book by explaining the law of attraction and manifesting. It is my intention that people who have read this book will be able to put it to practical use immediately and start attracting good things into their lives.

—Dr. David Che, Florida

Total Law
of
Attraction

Chapter 1

⌒

It All Starts with Your Beliefs

A belief is not merely an idea that the mind possesses; it is an idea that possesses the mind.

— Robert Bolton

I have to start this book with beliefs, because beliefs are at the deep core of the law of attraction and responsible for everything we experience in our lives. The word "believe" and its variants are so important that I am going to make them italic in the rest of this chapter. If you do not *believe* what I am teaching in this book, it is unlikely you would have purchased it, much less put the information to use.

Since birth, your life experiences have led you to *believe* certain things you hold to be true in your mind that have literally determined your present circumstances. Everyone's heard of the placebo effect, where someone is given what they think is a drug when it is actually just a sugar pill. In many cases the person reacts as if they were given the real drug. It's because they *believed* they were given the real thing! How many times in sports have you heard star athletes say, "No one thought we could win, but we *believed* in our ability to win."

I am a basketball fan and I've heard that comment too many

times to mention. You see very young people become millionaires these days. Older athletes in the Olympics are winning medals when people thought they didn't have a chance. How about former Senator Barack Obama running for president and being the first African American in US history to win the presidency when many people thought it was impossible? What do these individuals all have in common? It all started with their *belief* that it was possible! Whether it's presidential elections, sports, or anything, for that matter, what we believe directly determines our destiny. As you can see, beliefs are immensely powerful.

For you scientific people like me, who need more of a scientific explanation to support what I talked about above, here's one: In his book *The Holographic Universe* author Michael Talbot wrote about the work of neurophysiologist Karl Pribram. Based on Pribram's work, it says that visual information entering our brain is edited by our temporal lobes (next to our ears) before it is passed to the actual visual center of the brain. Pribram and his colleagues noted that less than 50 percent of what we see is based on information entering our eyes from physical objects. The other 50 percent plus is put together out of what we expect the world should look like. So, whatever image is entering our brain from the outside, our brains modify at least half of that based on our core beliefs. This, combined with the other 50 percent, is ultimately what we *see* in our own reality.

I am going to return to this powerful concept about *believing* in the later chapter on manifesting.

Chapter 2

The Law of Attraction and Quantum Physics

Quantum physics? What's that you say? Many of the books I've seen about the law of attraction use quantum physics to help explain and prove the law of attraction. That's great and I will use it too. However, these books don't ever talk about what quantum physics even *is*. When we hear the words "quantum physics," we think a bunch of really smart guys developed it, so we just accept it. For the many people who've never taken a physics course, much less quantum physics (it's usually a third-year course even for a physics major), I feel a short history is necessary.

We have all heard of Isaac Newton, the brilliant guy who developed classical physics in the late 1600s. This is the kind of physics where you can calculate, say, the speed of everyday objects in the natural world. Around the mid-1800s to the time scientists were building the atom bomb, it was discovered that Newton's physics didn't work for extremely tiny objects, such as atoms. That was when the field of quantum physics was born. Quantum physics allowed scientists to accurately calculate the behavior of very small particles. For our purposes here, since we can't visibly see atoms, think of them as being in an IMAGINARY world relative to us. QUANTUM PHYSICS DEALS WITH THE IMAGINARY WORLD.

To effectively explain the law of attraction and manifestation, I do need to start at the beginning with some very BASIC quantum stuff. Don't worry; I will be brief and I'll keep it as simple as possible.

～

Virtually everyone knows of Albert Einstein. He contributed a lot to modern science, but the one thing he is most famous for is an equation: $E = MC^2$. I think everyone at one time or another has seen this equation. Simply, it means energy can be changed into matter, and matter can be changed into energy. Matter is every physical thing you see in the world. Matter can be converted to energy, and energy can be turned into mass. In other words, mass and energy are the same thing, just in different forms. All matter you see is not really solid. It is all vibrating as energy, just at different rates of vibration. Your thoughts are waves of energy. They are similar to the waves of energy that your cell phone picks up from the tower, the signal your FM radio picks up, or radio transmissions between two people. Just because you can't visibly see thoughts as waves of energy doesn't mean they don't exist. The same is true when you use your cell phone. You can't see the signal the tower transmits to your phone, but you know it exists because you use it every day!

Your thoughts from your brain, whether positive or negative, create an emotional response in all the millions of cells in your body, which results in a powerful bodily vibration. If it's a positive emotion, the vibration is high. If it's a negative emotion, the vibration is low.

Okay, enough of that. Maybe you've read the different books on the law of attraction, but if you've only heard of it, here's a quick lesson: What you think about and focus on, you attract toward yourself. Actually, that's the definition you'll see in most other books and videos. I'd like to reword that so it's much more accurate: What you constantly FEEL AND THINK about, and consistently focus on, you attract into your life.

In the 1950s, Earl Nightingale, the famous motivational speaker, said, "We become what we think about." Let me reword that so it's a bit more accurate: "We become what we consistently think about." Just thinking about something doesn't necessarily cause it to show up in your life. It's the consistent thought of it that it shows up in your circumstances over time.

There are tons of self-help books out there on positive thinking, but have you noticed that people who've read them will tell you that they rarely, if ever, work?

The reason they don't is that it doesn't have a lot to do with what you think. It has much more to do with what you FEEL. Yes, your thoughts do play their part in determining how you feel, but here's the key:

{ Secret 1 }

Your FEELINGS, NOT your thoughts, determine what
you attract into your life.

In the physical world, opposites attract. Male and female, north and south pole of magnets, and the like . . . but when it comes to the laws of attraction and emotion, LIKE VIBRATIONS ATTRACTS THE SAME LIKE VIBRATIONS. Quantum physics has proven this. There's something called string theory (don't worry about the name) in quantum physics that says everything in the universe is just strands of vibrating energy. Every single thing we see is vibrating at its own speed and attracts to it another thing that is vibrating at the *same* speed. For our purposes though, here's what you need to know:

If you CHOOSE to think good thoughts and FEEL positive emotions, you'll have a HIGH rate of vibration and will gradually attract good circumstances into your life. Likewise, if you choose to think negative thoughts and FEEL negative emotions, your body has a LOW rate of vibration and you will gradually attract negative circumstances into your life. It's really just that simple!

Have you ever met someone and felt they had a good VIBE? You were attracted and probably wanted to associate with that person. On the other hand, have you met someone and felt a bad VIBE? You probably wanted to STAY AWAY from that person! Now that you understand the law of attraction, feeling good or bad VIBES isn't just a figure of speech.

Have you ever noticed that people who constantly bring their problems to the office, wanting everyone to know their issues and feeling negative all the time, have bad things that keep happening to them for no apparent reason? Well, it's because they keep focusing on negative thoughts, which creates negative feelings. As a result, they keep attracting negative circumstances into their lives according to the law of attraction. Most of the time people attract bad luck into their circumstances from a negative thought/feeling they had in the past that is showing up now.

I really want to stress Secret 1 because it's possible for you to think positive and still feel negative about something and vice versa. This is where the books about positive thinking fall short. If you think positive and feel bad, you'll still end up attracting negative things. The reverse is also true. I'm sure you can think of a few situations, but I have one that will drive the point home.

I'll use money as an example, because everyone can relate to money. Let's say you're short of it. You keep thinking to yourself, "I want more money." According to the law of attraction, what you keep focusing on and thinking about, you'll get. So shouldn't you be attracting more money? Not really. The reason is, when you keep thinking about wanting more money, what you're actually FEELING is a LACK of money. Since the feeling is lack, and feelings ultimately determine what you attract, you'll get more LACK in your life! It's a subtle meaning, and not touched upon in other books I've read on this subject. That's why books on positive thinking fail most of the time. What you should do is think to yourself that you have money AND train yourself to FEEL that you have money even though right now you might not have much. I admit this is not an easy thing to do at first. But it's how you'll gradually attract more money into your circumstances.

The law of attraction is really a law of DEFAULT. Meaning, if you see good circumstances around you, you tend to feel good and attract good things to yourself. If you see negative things around you, you tend to feel bad and likewise attract negative things. The law of attraction is JUST LIKE the law of gravity. It is working on you whether you're aware of it or not. When you don't understand gravity and don't know how to work with it, everything stays right on the ground. When you understand it, you can do great things, such as build a rocket that can escape gravity and go into outer space. It's the same with the law of attraction. You can live your life just blindly going along with the flow of good or bad circumstances, or you can understand it and work with it so you can focus on bringing more positive things into your life and minimize the negative things.

Note: Some other books teach that once you understand the law of attraction and start creating what you want by decision instead of by default; you're not using the law of attraction anymore but the law of deliberate creation. This is true. However, to keep things simple and to prevent confusion, I will keep referring to this as the law of attraction.

Chapter 3

The Conscious and Subconscious Minds: What They Are and How They Work

We all have one brain, but actually two separate minds in us. The mind that you are using to read this book right now is your Conscious mind. The area where your long-term memories, beliefs, and habits are stored is in your Subconscious mind. For our purposes, think of your Conscious mind as located in your brain and the Subconscious mind as located in your heart. (Other books will mention a third mind, the Superconscious. To keep things simple, since the Subconscious and Superconscious generally work together, I will limit myself to talking about just the Conscious and Subconscious.)

The two minds use different methods for communication. The Conscious mind works through logic and reasoning. It knows what is real and what isn't and has a good concept of time. The Subconscious mind works through strong emotion and repetition. It does not know what is real or what isn't, and it does not have a concept of time. The past, present, and future are all the same to the Subconscious mind. The Subconscious mind is basically opposite to the Conscious mind. These are all extremely important points that you must grasp and understand now, as they will be brought up numerous times throughout this book.

{ Secret 2 }

The Conscious mind CHOOSES WHAT you think about, but it is actually the Subconscious mind that brings it into your physical reality.

The Subconscious mind is present in every living being and is very powerful. We all have it. It has the amazing ability to gradually shape your outer environment and ATTRACT the things you are in VIBRATION with to you (remember the last chapter?).

*Everything you've attracted into your present circumstances has been the work of your Subconscious mind at one time or another, although you might not have been consciously aware of it.

Have you ever heard the saying: "When the HEART and MIND are working together, anything is possible?" I didn't fully understand it when I first heard it. What it means is that when your Subconscious (heart) is working together as a team with your Conscious (mind), you can accomplish most anything. If you look at how people behave in life, you'll see how this is true. When people fail to quit smoking, it's because their Conscious mind wants them to, but the ingrained habitual patterns in their Subconscious mind prevent them from doing so. On the flip side, let's say someone feels excited in their heart (Subconscious) about undertaking a new project or endeavor, and their logical (Conscious) mind tells them that it's completely possible, it's very likely they will accomplish it.

So the trick to manifesting anything into our lives is to have our Conscious and Subconscious working TOGETHER. But before I get into that, it is necessary to explain just exactly HOW our thoughts and emotions are transformed into physical reality. That will be explained in the next chapter.

Chapter 4

The ETHER in Space: UNLIMITED Manifestation Energy

This chapter will seem somewhat complicated, because I will be using a bit more of quantum physics. But I am going to do my best to make it easy to understand. You may have to reread this chapter again to get a better understanding of the important concepts.

I am going to go back to our Conscious and Subconscious minds in a moment, but first, I need to talk about the Ether in space. Are you ready?

Okay, you've seen pictures of the earth from outer space. Have you noticed that there is so much EMPTY space between the earth, moon, and stars? Even though it all seems like empty space, it really isn't empty at all. It's full of WAVES of invisible energy. This seemingly empty space, which is actually full of energy waves, has been called the Ether in some books. (Although science will say it's been proven no such Ether exists, you'll have to put aside that notion and firmly believe it to be true.)

If you've ever come across the famous book *The Science of Getting Rich* by Wallace Wattles, Ether is referred to as Thinking Stuff or Formless Substance. In religions, this could be referred to as God or the universal power. From now on, I will use the terms Ether and universal power interchangeably.

Whatever it is called, know that the empty space is actually filled with an endless (infinite) number of waves of energy. In quantum physics, these are called probability waves. I know this sounds deep, but stay with me.

Remember, in chapter 2, when I talked about how energy can be changed into matter and matter to energy? Well, these waves of energy in space can be changed into physical matter. How, you say? The answer is simple: Our thoughts can change those waves of energy into physical matter. Let me repeat:

{ Secret 3 }

Over time, our thoughts change the invisible waves of
energy in space into visible physical matter. It's true!

The reason why the waves of energy in space also have the word "probability" attached to them is because until a human mind has impressed his or her thought of something specific into the sea of wave energy, it is all just a bunch of wave energy with no form. Think of it this way: Imagine a blank piece of paper in front of you. On this blank piece of paper, you have an endless number of things you can visualize in your mind and draw on the paper. Let's say you decide to draw a car. Or say you decide to draw a house. No matter what you decide to draw on this piece of paper, if you think about it, those were all possibilities on this piece of paper *before* you even had the thought about the house or car. Does that make sense?

In the case of all the waves of energy in space, they are all probabilities because those waves can be changed into any physical form by the thought of a person. Here is an important point to make: Every single physical thing you see in front of you, such as cars, books, buildings, furniture, and the like, were all at one time a probability wave. They were originally created from the waves of energy through the thought of some living person. More important, all those physical things were ALREADY a probability, even BEFORE someone thought them into existence.

In science class, specifically chemistry, you're taught there are many different elements that make up all the different things in our physical world. In actuality, by saying all matter is energy and energy is matter, we can greatly simplify things and say all the different elements that make up all the different things we see in the world are basically different forms of just ONE element. That one element is the Ether-thinking substance—formless substance, or whatever you call it—it is all the SAME.

Now that you have a basic understanding of these concepts, we can now turn our attention to just how our mind creates physical reality by way of the Ether.

Chapter 5

—

How the Conscious and Subconscious Minds Create Physical Reality Through the Ether

Finally, we're able to get through the theories and on to the good stuff. I'm about to give you a modern, to-the-point explanation of just how our minds create physical reality through our thoughts.

You first use your Conscious mind, the one you are reading this book with right now, to think of something. It could be a car, a house, a new job, or anything, for that matter. It would be so easy if your Conscious mind could give this thought directly to the Ether in space and your desire would just materialize. But it doesn't work that way.

> Your Subconscious has the unlimited ability to bring you
> almost anything you wish for.

What happens is, you must be in a relaxed state first. In a relaxed state, this thought you have is transferred down to your Subconscious mind. Your Subconscious mind then sends this thought energy up into the Ether. As it moves up, it gets less dense. Once it enters the Ether, it converts what was once probability wave energy into a definite particle located at a position in space. Like a cloud gathering moisture, this particle attracts similar vibrational energies until it becomes dense enough, returns to the physical world, and shows up in your circumstances.

Many people will ask, "Why can't our Conscious mind give our thoughts directly to the Ether?" That's a good question. And the answer is, your Conscious mind is like a guardian or protector. It is a built-in safety mechanism for you. Imagine if every single thought you had manifested into physical reality! All your bad thoughts, in addition to your good thoughts, would show up in your life. You wouldn't want that, would you?

Your Subconscious is like an Aladdin's lamp, except that unlike Aladdin's lamp, you're not limited to just three wishes. Your Subconscious has the unlimited ability to bring you almost anything you wish for. But our creator made sure we had a guardian for our Subconscious so that things don't get out of control. He didn't want us to manifest every little thing we thought about. That could be like opening Pandora's box!

Now, I could say "that's it" to how manifestation works with our minds. But as you and I both know, there's much more to the process. There are a lot of other SUBTLE, not so obvious principles involved with manifesting that many other books leave out. Miss a step, and it's like baking a cake and not adding sugar. It won't work. I will explain these subtle principles in detail in the next chapters.

Chapter 6

The Not-So-Obvious Concepts in Manifesting (Part 1)

I am going to go more into detail about what I discussed in chapter 5 because there are a lot of additional small details that I need mention for all of this to work.

First, to manifest something, you have to have a burning DESIRE for it. You have to REALLY WANT it! Anything that you would like to have or isn't a true heart's desire will NOT likely manifest. It must be a genuine true heart's desire. You can tell whether it's your real heart's desire or not by seeing if you have to make excuses in your mind why you may NOT be able to get it. A real heart's desire requires NO excuses. You want it no matter what it takes!

I touched on this in the last chapter, but in order for your Conscious mind to impress upon your Subconscious mind with your thought, you must be in a relaxed state. That allows the transfer to take place. So once you're in a relaxed state, you start to think about what it is you desire. You need to clear your mind of other things and just focus on this. It's not as easy as you think! Everyone in the beginning will tend to have many distracting thoughts. In time, you will get better with practice.

Okay, now close your eyes and visualize your desire as if it were a movie in your mind. Think of yourself as the director in a movie. Now comes the next and extremely important step. You MUST add strong EMOTION to your visualization! Look at the word: "emotion." It is E-motion = Energy in Motion!

{ Secret 4 }

You have to mentally see your desire as if you already have it, and truly FEEL how it is you would feel if you already had what you desired.

In chapter 3, I said that the Subconscious has no way of telling what is real and what isn't. It also has no concept of time. I also said emotion is the language of the Subconscious mind. When you think of something you desire, and impress it upon your Subconscious mind with emotion, your Subconscious does not know if it's real or not. It doesn't care. It just accepts what you give it and starts to do its work.

Here's another very important point:

{ Secret 5 }

There is no need to think about HOW you will obtain your desire. You only need to visualize, with emotion THE END RESULT. Your Subconscious will find the means to bring it to you without your logical Conscious mind even being aware of it.

For example, if you desire to successfully close a business deal or start a new business, visualize a picture in your mind that shows ONLY the critical point at the stage where the FINAL successful act is done. You don't need to worry about how it will be accomplished. That's the beauty of the process.

Lifting a book off a table requires energy. The same is true for your thought to enter the Ether of space. Once your Conscious mind gives your thought to your Subconscious, the EMOTION your Subconscious mind adds to it gives it the energy required to send your thought UP into the Ether of space. Once that thought energy with emotion enters the Ether, it starts to change what was once invisible energy waves into definite particles.

~

*By visualizing repeatedly, with strong emotion and faith, on a day-by-day basis, these particles slowly begin to materialize into the object of your desire and will eventually show up in your circumstances. Remember, the Subconscious is affected by EMOTION and REPETITION.

I need to elaborate on Secret 4. When you close your eyes and see your desire in your mind, you have to be as detailed as possible and see your desire as if you already have it, NOT as if you want it. There's a BIG difference. For example, if you desire a new car, see yourself as if in a movie DRIVING the car. Don't see yourself wanting the car. If it's a new house, see yourself living in it ALREADY. Don't see yourself standing on the side of the road wishing you could have it.

The details and being specific are really important. If it's a new car, see in your mind the exact color, make, and model of the car. If it's a house, see in your mind the exact size, color, style, of what you'd like. If it's a certain amount of money you need, see in your mind receiving the EXACT amount. If you just visualize yourself getting more money, your Subconscious won't be able to understand it. More money can mean $100, $1,000, or $10,000. You need to be specific. If it's a new job you'd like, see yourself doing not just any job, just that *specific* job. The clearer and more specific your visualization is with strong emotion, the higher the chance you will receive what you want.

Your Subconscious creates exactly what you give it. If you give it a picture of wanting or wishing for something, that's just what you'll keep getting—more circumstances of wanting or wishing for it! When you visualize, with emotion, yourself already having it, you're basically "TRICKING" your Subconscious mind into bringing you what you want. You already know the Subconscious has no concept of time or what is real and what isn't. It is like the genie. It does exactly what its master or guardian—in this case your Conscious mind, tells it to do.

Visualizing your desire with emotion should NOT be a long process. All it should really take is about five to ten quality minutes. Any longer and your mind may start to wander. From now on, I will refer to what I described above as a major manifestation session.

A major manifestation session defined is: When you relax yourself in a quiet environment, clear your mind, close your eyes, and clearly visualize with strong EMOTION in your mind, a picture of yourself ALREADY having and feeling what you desire for about five to ten minutes.

For real results, you must faithfully do a major manifestation session at most twice a day, every single day, until you start seeing evidence of your desire starting to manifest in your circumstances.

Chapter 7

The Not-So-Obvious Concepts in Manifesting (Part 2)

When your Subconscious sends your thought into the Ether, your thought energy attracts similar vibrations and, once they are dense enough, returns to you.

Now, let's say you visualized a new car. It's not like a new car just appears right away out of thin air, as you see in magic shows. It doesn't work that way. There is always a time delay from the moment you visualize something to when you start to see it in your physical reality. This time delay factor is the main reason why many people don't believe in the law of attraction and why they cannot associate thought with creating reality. But that's the way it really is.

*The reason behind this time delay is that our thought energy is still in the energy form. The energy form is not as DENSE as physical matter. It takes time for our thought energy to get transformed into the denser physical matter we can see with our eyes.

Your Subconscious mind is at least a thousand times more powerful than your Conscious mind. It brings your desire not immediately out of thin air, but by a gradual route. If you had visualized a new business, you might get a sudden flash of INTUITION on how to go about starting it.

{ Secret 6 }

You must learn to completely TRUST your
INTUITION (gut feeling) over your logical mind and
take action when necessary!

This is extremely important. Your logical Conscious mind, that little voice in your head, might tell you NOT to go ahead with something. But if you have that impulsive, gut feeling, you must learn to trust your HEART. This flash of intuition isn't just a random thought you had. It is something you had visualized previously that has returned and is trying to manifest into your reality. Do not pass it up! Incidentally, many great discoveries in scientific history were made this way.

To use the car example again, your Subconscious might make it so you'll get something in the mail about a huge sale on the car you want. Or maybe the TV stations you watch will keep showing commercials for this car and the special rates dealers are offering on it. While your logical Conscious mind can think of only one or maybe two ways you can obtain this car, your Subconscious mind is connected with the infinite power of the Ether intelligence above and knows of many different ways it can bring it to you. You have to TRUST your Subconscious instead of your logical mind, which will tell you otherwise.

Chapter 8

Why BELIEVING Makes ALL the Difference in the World!

Remember the first chapter on beliefs? I talked about how at least 50 percent of the world we see is based on our beliefs. Let's go back to it now and see why it is perhaps the single most important principle behind the law of attraction and manifestation.

On the surface, it seems like believing in something is purely a motivational thing. When you hear a coach tell his or her athletes they need to believe in themselves to succeed, it would appear that it's all just motivational, with little scientific basis.

However, when you start looking closer, nothing can be further from the truth. When you watch movies about sports heroes, you always see how someone faces hardship by losing in the beginning, only to come back later to gloriously win it all because they completely changed their attitude and believed in themselves. It's very inspirational to watch.

Here's what I'm getting at on a scientific level regarding the law of attraction and the power of BELIEVING: After you do a major manifestation session (chapter 6), you have to continue to sustain the BELIEF in your heart that what you visualized is TRUE. Remember how I said before that it's your FEELINGS that have the REAL power to attract what you want? Your FEELINGS affect the rate at which your body vibrates, and it is the sustained feeling of BELIEF that puts you in a vibrational match with your desire, thus attracting your desire to you at a certain time as determined by your Subconscious mind.

When it comes to the law of attraction, most people have the attitude "I'll believe it when I see it." And that's the very reason they'll never get the law of attraction to ever work for them. The truth is, "You'll see it when you believe it!"

{ Secret 7 }

When you're visualizing your desire, truly BELIEVE it
when you see it in your mind.

AFTER visualizing your desire, always think to yourself, "I'll see it in time if I keep BELIEVING it." That way, you're always in the right state of perfect vibration.

⌒

*The sustained feeling of 100 percent BELIEF in your desire as being true in your Conscious mind before you see any physical evidence of it is perhaps the single most important part of making the law of attraction work successfully. I cannot stress this point enough. When you have gasoline, a single spark is necessary to ignite it. By the same analogy, a continuous sustained belief that your desire is truly real in your Conscious mind, after you visualize it, is the spark that will ignite your Subconscious mind to start working to bring it to you!

⌒

*I want to emphasize that the law of attraction is always working, whether someone believes in it or not. People who don't believe in the law of attraction will live their life by default. They go with the flow of good or bad circumstances. People who understand the law of attraction and APPLY it live their life by DESIGN. Because they BELIEVE it, they work with the law of attraction to change their circumstances AT WILL.

> Jesus said to him, If you can believe, all things are possible to him who believes.
>
> —Mark 9:23

> Therefore I tell you, whatever you ask for in prayer, BELIEVE that you have received it, and it will be yours.
>
> —Mark 11:24

When you truly BELIEVE in your heart, you can ACHIEVE, RECEIVE, and SUCCEED!

Chapter 9

⌒

The Law of Detachment

The number 9 is a special number in numerology. The ancients considered the number 9 to be the number of perfection and harmony. I reserved the number 9 for this chapter to thoroughly discuss the law of detachment because it is extremely important. Most books NEVER mention, much less discuss, the law of detachment, and yet it is a HUGE reason why the law of attraction fails for most people. This concept may be hard to understand at first, which is why I am going to spend a good deal of time on it.

Everyone has seen the Chinese yin-yang symbol. It represents the dual nature of the universe. Everything in the universe has its direct opposite. The male/female, light/dark, sun/moon, negative/positive charges, etc. . . . you get the idea. If the law of attraction is the yin, then the law of detachment is the yang. Equal but opposite in importance.

I remember when I was nineteen years old I was given what was regarded as the highest book in Buddhism. It was called *The Heart Sutra*. Before opening the book, I glanced at the back cover to get a brief idea what this book was about. It said, "The beneficial function of the Heart Sutra is the eradication of your attachments. We cannot be at ease because we have impediments. If you have no impediments you can be at ease. . . ." (BTTS, 1980). I never understood the true meaning of that until I started deeply studying the law of attraction. What it means for our purposes is this: To receive anything from the Ether (or formless substance) that we visualize and desire, we have to be completely DETACHED from it.

Another way of saying it is, even though what you visualized is your true heart's desire, when you're not visualizing it, you have to treat it as something that you DO NOT HAVE TO HAVE to be happy. You feel happy regardless, and you don't really need what you want.

For example, let's say there's this car you want. You visualized it with emotion down to the last detail. You believe that it's already on its way to you. But at the same time, you have to have this feeling of DETACHMENT. You have to have the feeling that you don't need this car to be happy. You're not attached to it.

You would apply this in the same way whether it was an object you desire, a particular situation, event, or circumstance. If a negative situation arises along the way that isn't what you visualized and expected, you would think to yourself, "This isn't what I expected. But who cares? I'm confident something better will come along." This is extremely important to keep in mind.

Now realize being DETACHED does NOT mean you don't have any desire, feel anything, or have no emotions. You still have desires, but you're not attached to your desires. It also means you don't keep dwelling in your mind on that one thing or circumstance because you didn't get it or it doesn't go your way. You have to have a carefree attitude. You LET IT GO.

Let me talk about the Subconscious mind for a moment. I didn't mention this before, but I will now. Remember how emotions are the language of the Subconscious mind? The number one enemy of the Subconscious mind is the emotion of FEAR. Fear hurts the Subconscious mind and prevents it from working properly. The other enemies of the Subconscious are doubt, worry, and lack of confidence.

Attachment to your desire is an emotion of FEAR. Attachment

basically means three things: One, you're afraid of losing something you already have. Two, you're afraid of not getting something you really want. Three, you're afraid of getting something you DON'T want. Whichever it is, when you're attached, it's an underlying feeling of FEAR. This feeling of fear disables your Subconscious mind and gives that same message to the Ether (formless substance). The Ether interprets your feeling of attachment as a state of LACK. As a result, you don't get what you want and/or you attract what you don't want. When you train yourself to become completely DETACHED from your desires or a particular outcome for that desire to appear, the Ether interprets this as you ALREADY have what you want and will bring about the circumstances for you to receive it.

{ Secret 8 }

It seems like a paradox, but it's true: When you don't have to have anything and can let it all go (detachment), you can get everything.

Detachment is the most difficult skill to learn and apply. But at the same time, it is THE MOST important skill you need to master if you are serious about attracting what you want. If you really think about it, all suffering in the world comes from some form of attachment. Name any bad situation and you can always trace it back to attachment. Let's say I get a brand-new car and I accidentally wreck it the next day. If I was attached, I would moan over it and be constantly miserable. If I was detached, I would maybe feel negative for a moment, but then I would realize that worrying about it won't change anything. So I let it go and move on to better things.

Whether it's loved ones who pass away, wars over resources or religion, loss of property or possessions, arguments . . . it all can be traced back to attachment of something that is causing those negative feelings. When we are unhappy with certain people because of the way they are, we need to understand that it is because we are

ATTACHED to the fact that they must conform to our own personal standards. When they don't conform to our standard, we get unhappy about it. If we detach ourselves from this and just learn to accept our family, friends, relatives, and even enemies for what they are instead of always thinking of a way to try to change them to the way we think they should be, then we can be happy!

It's not easy. But once we train ourselves to detach and let go, we can obtain two powerful benefits:

1. We FEEL happy and at ease no matter what the situation, thus continuously attracting good things to ourselves.
2. By feeling happy and calm, we can effectively use the law of attraction and visualization to get what we want.

Now I understand what that ancient Buddhist book was teaching all along. Being in a state of detachment is the ultimate state to be in. This is the state the Buddha, Jesus, and other ascended masters attained. Being detached means being free!

Chapter 10

The Law of Detachment and the Uncertainty Principle

Wait a sec, the uncertainty principle? Did I scare you with some big words? Don't worry. It will all make sense.

So what does the uncertainty principle have to do with the law of attraction and manifestation? Everything! Although you really don't have to know this principle to make things work, it is still very important that you have some understanding of it so you know why you must be DETACHED from your desire if you are to ever attract it into your life.

In 1927, the German physicist Werner Heisenberg formulated what is known as the uncertainty principle for microscopic (very small) particles. Werner Heisenberg was a brilliant Nobel Prize–winning physicist who would later head Germany's atomic bomb project in World War II. Some say he deliberately halted the project due to his moral conscience, but that's another story.

Anyway, I will first define what Heisenberg's uncertainty principle is, then I will explain what it has to do with the law of detachment.

Basically, Heisenberg's uncertainty principle goes like this: When trying to measure the position and speed of a microscopic particle, you CANNOT know both at the same time. That is to say, when you know the position of a particle, you can't know its speed. The more you try to know its speed, the less you'll know its position. Now let me explain how this concept ties together directly with the law of detachment.

If you remember in chapter 5, once your thought plus emotional energy enters the Ether, it changes what was once an energy wave in the Ether into a particle located at a specific position in space. Okay, so now during your visualization, you have established your desire as a microscopic particle in space at a particular location.

Allow me to sidetrack for just a moment. Typically, after everyone visualizes something, they often ask themselves, "How and when is my desire going to manifest?" Or if it's been some time and nothing seems to have happened after they have continued to visualize something, they will often wonder, "It's not working; why hasn't my desire manifested yet? How or when is it going to arrive?"

Now let's go back to the uncertainty principle and apply it to a visualization: When you have established your thought visualization as a particle at a particular position in space, you cannot know its speed. That is to say, you cannot know how or when the speed will manifest. The more you try to think about how or when it will show up, the more you will actually push your desire away and the less likely you will receive your desire.

To put it simply, once you have closed your eyes and strongly visualized your desire with emotion for five to ten minutes, you have to do your best to completely forget about it right after you visualized it. This is so important, I have to repeat it: The more you keep thinking about what you just visualized or the more you try to think about how or when your desire will arrive, the less the chance your desire will come to you. If you've ever had past experience with this, the uncertainty principle is the reason you usually receive your desire at a time when you're least expecting or thinking about it.

I know it all sounds counterintuitive. You get what you want when you can give up your attachment to it and usually (not always) at the moments you're thinking about it THE LEAST. Remember, attachment is perhaps the number one cause (next to lack of belief) why the law of attraction and manifestation do NOT end up working for people.

To list it out simply, attachment is:

1. Thinking about your desire all the time after you've visualized it.
2. Constantly wondering how and when you will receive your desire.
3. Persistently thinking you need your desire to be happy.

It's not easy in the beginning, but you have to train yourself to detach if you are ever going to make the law of attraction and manifestation work for you.

DETACHMENT means:

1. You ONLY think about your desire during the times you are visualizing it.
2. You don't give an ounce of thought or worry to how and when your desire is going to manifest. You surrender and completely trust the universe.
3. You think it would be nice to have what you desire, but you don't really, in your heart, need it to be happy.

Treat visualization like a light switch. A light switch turns a light either on or off. There is no in between with a light switch. That is the same way you should visualize. If you visualize your desire two times a day, visualize it intensely with emotion and then completely put it out of your mind until the next time you visualize it. That's the key.

Here's another example. Say you want to pass three hours' worth of time. What's faster, staring at a clock for three hours or engaging in a fun activity for three hours? Obviously, doing the activity! When you stare at a clock, you're chasing after time, and time passes very slowly. When you're having fun, time is catching up to you. Using the same analogy, if you visualize your desire and keep thinking how or when it's going to come to you, you're chasing after it, so it will come to you very slowly . . . often, not at all. But when you forget about it right after you visualize it, your Subconscious is free to do its work and your desire will come toward you passively.

Reread this chapter again, if needed, to fully understand it. When you faithfully combine the law of attraction WITH the law of detachment on a daily basis, you are certain to see the positive results of your labor at the times you LEAST expect it.

Chapter 11

*

Express GRATITUDE for Everything in Life!

Do you remember the last time you gave something to someone or did a good deed for someone and they expressed gratitude to you for it? You felt good even though you didn't expect anything in return, didn't you? If that person asked you for something else, you would have likely given it to them too.

On the other hand, do you remember how you felt when you gave something or did a good deed for someone and they took it for granted and weren't grateful? Most of us would not feel as happy and would not likely go out of our way to do the same thing for that person again.

It is the same with the law of attraction and manifestation. When you visualize your desire with great emotional intensity and BELIEVE it in your heart to be real, you should also sincerely say thank you and FEEL GRATEFUL right afterward. When you feel grateful and give thanks to the Ether (formless substance), it reacts by bringing you what you want.

In the real world, we say thanks when someone has done a good deed for us or when we receive something. So some might ask, "Why am I giving thanks when I haven't gotten what I want yet?"

Actually, when you visualize something in the beginning, it has already been created in the Ether, although it's in a weak state of existence. The more you visualize it, the stronger it becomes. But here's the secret:

{ Secret 9 }

It is the FEELING of gratitude that keeps your mind
connected with the intelligence of the universal creative
power! The key is to FEEL continuously grateful
BEFORE and after you receive your desire.

In fact, you should look around and also start feeling grateful for everything you already have around you. No matter what your current circumstance, you can feel grateful for being alive, where you live, your accomplishments, your possessions, your good moments . . . for everything! Being grateful is the HIGHEST state of happiness. One can be happy, but not necessarily grateful. But there's no way one can be grateful without being happy. And remember the law of attraction I first defined in chapter 2? Let me say it again here: "What you constantly FEEL AND THINK about, and consistently focus on, you attract into your life."

If you're constantly feeling grateful, which is the highest state of happiness, your body is vibrating at a very high frequency and you'll always be attracting good things. When you feel grateful toward your desire, the Ether or universal power responds (action/reaction) by giving you more of what you want.

I just opened a fortune cookie the other day and, talk about coincidence, was very surprised to see that the fortune said, "Gratitude is not only the greatest of virtues, but the parent of all others."

Jesus knew the secret of gratitude. Do you recall the story in the Bible where he fed five thousand people with five loaves and two fish? Here's the relevant part: "And he directed the people to sit down on the grass. Taking the five loaves and the two fish and looking UP to heaven, he GAVE THANKS and broke the loaves." You know the rest.

Is it coincidence that the word "attitude" rhymes with "gratitude"? According to the Merriam-Webster dictionary, attitude is defined as "a: a mental position with regard to a fact or state, b: a feeling or emotion toward a fact or state." Well then, here's something to keep in mind all the time: The BEST attitude is an ATTITUDE of GRATITUDE!

Combining the law of attraction, the law of detachment, and now gratitude, I can reveal to you the ultimate state of mind to be at to obtain the highest level of happiness in life. It doesn't matter what book or ancient text you'll ever read. It all comes back to this truth: Train yourself to *be attached to nothing. Be grateful for everything.* If you can train yourself to do this, you cannot fail to see amazing changes in your life day by day.

Chapter 12

Being AWARE of Negative Possibilities PREVENTS Them from Happening

The concept I will present here is virtually never talked about in other law of attraction books. Yet it is very important, so it deserves its own chapter.

All law of attraction books teach us that if we always think and feel positive we will attract positive things to us. For the most part, that is true. But it does leave one crucial thing out, which is: How do we prevent negative things from happening to us?

Realize that every single human on earth is under the power of the law of attraction, whether they realize it or not, just like we're all under gravity's power. However, not every person understands the law of attraction, so they're probably living their life in default. If they happen to constantly feel and think negative, they will be attracting negative circumstances. Sometimes, if you happen to be around a person or persons who are attracting negative things, you might get caught up in the middle of something negative. Obviously, the best thing to do is avoid being around negative people in general. But there are situations where you cannot avoid a potentially negative situation. We already know how to continuously attract positive things to us. So how do we prevent bad things from happening to us?

Here's the secret: BE AWARE OF THEM.

Okay, before you start thinking that I'm contradicting the law of attraction, listen to what I have to say.

Being aware of something does not mean you dwell upon or constantly think about it. Being aware means thinking about it for only a split second, without any emotion. Thoughts of this nature don't go through the whole Conscious/Subconscious thing. Split-second awareness thoughts go straight into the Ether and are actually frozen there. Split-second awareness stops potential physical reality from manifesting.

For example, if I'm driving down the highway and I see a truck in front of me carrying lots of loose gravel, I don't want the gravel to come flying out all over my car and scratching the heck out of it. So, what I would do is think of the gravel actually flying out and hitting my car for a split second. Because it's only for a split second, I don't have any emotion associated with it, so it doesn't go through my Subconscious and get created into my reality.

How many times in your life can you recall being aware of something negative? You took the precaution of getting a spare tire for your car, yet you've never used it. But there are also times where you were feeling and thinking positive. Then something negative happened that you did not at all expect, such as driving around with no spare, thinking/feeling all positive, not thinking at all about anything that could possibly go wrong, and then you end up getting a flat.

This is why young adults easily get into accidents. In their teens and early twenties, young people are feeling independent and happy, and thus attract positive things. But many think they're invincible and never give much thought to anything negative that might happen to them. When these events do happen, they're at loss to explain why.

Now that you understand that split-second awareness actually stops reality in its tracks, you can see from the previous chapter why you have to be detached and completely forget about your desire right after you visualize it. When you're not doing a major manifestation session (end of chapter 6), being constantly aware of your desire actually stops it from happening. The LESS aware you are of what you just visualized, the EASIER it will manifest into your reality.

You can't completely eliminate all negative things from ever happening to you, but you can MINIMIZE them by being AWARE of them.

Chapter 13

Never See the World the Same Way Again

If you haven't figured out by now that everything you see around you in your physical world is all made originally from thought energy, let me say it clearly right now.

{ Secret 10 }

EVERYTHING you see in the physical world originated
at one time from the thought energy of a living being.

And here's something else. The Ether, or formless substance in space, we discussed before that is filled with wave energy is ENDLESS. There is easily more than enough many times over to go around for every living being on earth. We're always trying out of ignorance to compete with the business next door, trying to get a bigger piece of the pie. In reality, when you understand how to create reality at will by your thought energy, you'll see that there's no need for competition.

We can acquire all we desire by applying all the information and techniques I've explained in the previous chapters.

Do you remember in grade school when you learned about cause and effect? Well, let me make a simple but extremely powerful revelation here:

{ Secret 11 }

Every single physical object or event you see in the world IS
AN EFFECT. The true cause of all physical objects that
have ever come into being and events that occur all started
from THOUGHT.

To put it into a single sentence, everything visible to the eye is a physical EFFECT that originally came from a mental (mind) cause. Once
you understand this truth, you'll never look at the world the same
way again. You'll see that circumstances should NOT have the ability
to affect you. Sure, when you come into good circumstances, you feel
good. But when you happen to experience negative circumstances,
you have to train yourself to see the negative circumstance as just an
EFFECT. Learn to see that negative circumstances aren't really the
cause of anything. Once you do that, you can gradually think yourself into a positive situation.

I used the word "gradual" because many books just tell you to
think positive and that's it. That's only half the story. Well-focused
thoughts need TIME to gradually manifest into physical reality. You
have to be patient and PERSISTENT. If you put half the effort into a
certain thing, you'll only get half a result or no result at all.

What you need to do in times of unfavorable circumstances is to
first see the circumstance as ONLY an effect. Realize the TRUE cause
is from habitual PAST negative thoughts and immediately start to visualize yourself with emotion in a very positive situation every single
day without fail. DON'T dwell on what happened in the past, and
DON'T ponder over the future. Just focus only on the present moment and start to visualize with emotion a positive circumstance for
yourself. Once you do that faithfully single every day, you'll see that
the future will start to take care of itself.

There's a saying, "Yesterday is history. Tomorrow is a mystery.
Today is a gift. That's why it's called the present." For example, if your
business is slow and you want more customers coming in, continu-

ally visualize a lot of customers coming into your store every single day. Believe it and feel it to be true. In time, circumstances will slowly change to match your visualization. To your surprise, you may get more business. Or you might get a flash of intuition to add and/or change something about your business, which will draw new customers in as a result.

After you have learned what this chapter has taught, you'll be able to "see" what people are thinking. Now, you obviously can't see thoughts. But you can see physical circumstances. If you ever want to know what someone is thinking, take a good look at their circumstances. Remember, everything you can visibly see are physical effects that originally came from mental (mind) thought. Although you can't directly see someone else's thoughts, you can see the condition of their circumstances. So indirectly you can see their habitual thoughts.

Chapter 14

Taking ACTION at the Right Time

This is the last and very critical step in the law of attraction process. When you follow the steps I have outlined throughout this book, as you've seen already, it requires a lot of mental thinking work. The truth is, the vast majority of the work necessary to bring your desire to you is already done during the mind visualization process. However, for you to fully activate the law of attraction, you still have to take necessary PHYSICAL action TOWARD your desire to RECEIVE it. You can't just sit around every day expecting your desire to just appear out of thin air right in front of you. As humans, we're not at the spiritual level to where things appear to us right after we think about them. As I said before, there is always a time delay to when we first visualize something, until it comes into our physical reality.

Notice I titled this chapter "Taking ACTION at the Right Time." I didn't just title it "Taking Action." There's a subtle but important difference between the two. Taking action means you're taking random action toward something without any sure sense of direction. This action is inefficient and results in a lot of unnecessary work on your part.

"Taking Action at the Right Time" is different. What this means is, after you've visualized your desire, it may seem like nothing is happening for some time. When this is the case, you should NOT have to do anything. You should ONLY take action when circumstances appear and seem to go in the direction TOWARD your desire OR when you get a flash of intuition that gives you the impulse to do something.

So, for example, let's say there's this new expensive television I want. After I've visualized it every day, it may seem like nothing is happening. So I don't do anything, but I keep visualizing it. Then I start seeing commercials on TV with special deals on that particular TV or I get flyers in the mail for huge sales on that TV. Well, that's a sign to me that I need to start taking ACTION toward my desire.

There are some other very important points I am going to review again here. As I said before, your Subconscious mind is at least a thousand times more powerful than your logical Conscious mind. When you visualize something you desire, your Conscious mind can only think of one or two ways you can get this thing. But your Subconscious mind knows MANY other ways to bring your desire to you that your logical Conscious mind wouldn't have the slightest clue about. In the case of the television, you could only think that by sale ads coming in the mail, you would go buy the television. But when your Subconscious goes to work, it could be that you have a close friend who knows someone else who is interested in selling the exact television you want at a great price! The point is, your Subconscious mind is connected with the Ether, or universal power. It is extremely intelligent and works the circumstances to bring you your desire in ways that your logical Conscious mind can't even imagine.

This also goes back to the law of detachment and why you have to completely forget about what you visualized before. When you want your Subconscious mind to go to work, you have to LET GO of your logical waking Conscious mind to let it do its job. The best way to do that is to FORGET about what you visualized RIGHT after you visualized it! It's like the cruise control in your car. You can't be on cruise control and manually drive the car at the same time. When you turn the cruise control on, your foot comes off the pedal and the car moves on its own. When you want to manually drive the car again, you turn the cruise control off.

You should treat your Subconscious mind as your car's cruise control and your Conscious mind as you, the driver. Right after you visualized your desire, you turned on the Subconscious mind (cruise control). Now let your desire go by completely forgetting about it with your Conscious mind (you, the driver) and let the Subconscious (cruise control) automatically do its work! Stop wondering how and when your desire is going to appear into your circumstances. Be detached, let it happen on its own, and take the necessary action when it appears it's coming toward you.

Keep in mind that once your desire presents itself and you're taking action toward it, THEN you can think about it as much as you'd like. It's the initial process where you have to temporarily put it out of your mind.

Let me make another important point about action, work, and effort. NOTHING IN THIS WORLD THAT IS WORTHWHILE COMES EASY. Everything that is worthwhile will take both a good amount of persistent, focused THINKING and necessary physical ACTION to accomplish. You have to do both. You cannot just intensely think about something but do no physical action. You can't NOT think about something and just go forward with action because that is a lot of wasted physical labor. You should let your mind do most of the work, and you physically step into the creation process at the appropriate time. That is the most efficient method.

If you wish to be a doctor and visualize yourself being a doctor, you still need to undergo years of diligent study (action) to become one. If you want to build a large building, you have to first visualize (think) about it, and still bring forth the necessary manpower (action) and means of constructing one.

If you desire more money, you should either visualize yourself in a higher paying job/profession, or visualize yourself starting a profitable small business. Money doesn't just appear out of thin air when you visualize it. The ACTION of setting up a business is the means by which you RECEIVE money. You EARN money by offering services that are in demand and of value to people.

For something to manifest in the physical world, it all must start with focused (not random) thought. Next, strong emotion is added to the thought. And finally, one must take appropriate (not random) action at the right moments to RECEIVE it.

{ Secret 12 }

When you combine PERSISTENT THOUGHT, STRONG emotion, emotion-sustained BELIEF, and massive ACTION AT THE RIGHT TIME, you are sure to receive your true heart's desire.

Here's an analogy of the process using a car as an example:

Thought (car) + Emotion (gasoline)

+

(100%) Sustained Belief
(constant sparks to ignite gasoline)

+

Action (driver)

RESULTS IN = MANIFESTATION
(car moves to destination)

Chapter 15

Putting It All Together into a Practical Method
of Manifestation

I promised from the beginning that I would take all the information about the law of attraction and manifestation and put it all into a practical, usable method suitable for daily use. You've read and understood all the theory behind this. It's very important that you understand some of the BASIC principles behind why things work the way they do besides just the practical techniques. When your logical CONSCIOUS mind BELIEVES things as true and gives that same message to your SUBCONSCIOUS mind, amazing things start to happen!

Okay, so let me simplify things as much as I can with this step-by-step summary:

1. You should visualize your desire at LEAST once a day. Ideally, you should visualize it at MOST twice a day, every single day for at least THIRTY STRAIGHT DAYS. This is how long it generally takes to train the Subconscious mind to something new. Not doing it for even just one day can set you back TEN days.

2. You should find a quiet room to visualize where you won't be disturbed for at least half an hour. This gives you time to settle your mind and allows you to think about what it is you want.

3. Know EXACTLY what you want down to the last detail. Be specific. Now visualize in your mind only the final outcome of your desire. Don't concern yourself with how you could receive your desire, only focus on the end result. The rest will take care of itself by way of coincidences.

4. Add strong EMOTION to the visualization. This is extremely important! This should take five to ten minutes.

5. End your visualization by either mentally "swallowing" the image in your mind inward or upward toward the sky.

6. *Do your best to forget about what you just visualized UNTIL the next time you visualize it. Let it go out of your Conscious awareness. The faster you let it go out of your mind, the more effective your visualization will be. You have to let go of your Conscious mind for your Subconscious mind to work.

7. You must maintain the BELIEF in your heart 100 percent that what you saw in your mind with emotion is true. Continue to BELIEVE that what you thought about is already in the creation process and on its way to you. You will, in time, see it if you sustain your belief in it.

8. Say to yourself, "Thank you," and feel grateful to the Ether (universal power) for being able to give you what you want. Don't take anything for granted, and FEEL grateful all the time for every little thing that you have. This keeps you connected with the universal power.

9. During the times you're not visualizing your desire, which is 98 percent of the time, learn to DETACH (let go) from your present negative circumstances and at the SAME time have a feeling of certainty (confidence) for the future. Also, resist the temptation to think about how or when your desire will manifest. It is not easy, but you need to train yourself to think that you really don't NEED your desire to be happy.

10. Your desire will manifest as coincidences (also known as synchronicities) and intuition. Take action, massive action, if necessary, when these opportunities show up. Trust your heart!

***11. You can also do a mini manifestation session at different times during the day. A mini manifestation session is when you LET GO, for a moment, your daily stresses of life. Then FEEL how you would feel if what you desire is already in your possession. Then put it out of your mind until you do another major or mini manifestation session.

The PADME Acronym: A Memory Aid

Over two thousand years ago, the Buddha was basically teaching the law of attraction when he taught that the mind is responsible for all physical existence. The highest mantra in Buddhism is "Om Mani Padme Hum." I took the second to last word, "Padme," and made an ACRONYM out of it so you can easily remember what to always keep in mind during the times you're NOT visualizing your desire, which is MOST of the time. I'm going to list and give a brief explanation of what each letter stands for:

P-ositive emotions throughout the day
A-wareness of negative possibilities
D-etachment
M-assive action toward your desire
E-xperience gratitude for everything

P-ositive emotions throughout the day. When you FEEL positive, your body is vibrating at a high level and you'll make it a habit to attract good things to you.

A-wareness of negative possibilities. Although you're attracting positive things to yourself by feeling good, you're NOT stopping potential negative things from happening. Be aware of potential negative possibilities for just a split second. Do NOT dwell on them.

D-etachment. You don't have to have the desire. Let it go. When you detach, you totally forget about the desire right after you visualize it. You don't worry about how or when it will happen. You don't even have to possess it to be happy. When you don't need it, that's when you can get it!

M-assive action toward your desire. For you to receive your desire in the physical world, you have to take physical action toward your desire when the opportunities present themselves in the form of either a physical coincidence, impulse to act, and/or intuition in your mind giving you new ideas.

E-xperience gratitude for everything. When you feel grateful for everything you already have and express gratitude to the universal power above before you even see physical evidence of your desire, you are connected to the universal power and your desire will be brought to you at the right time as determined by your Subconscious mind.

Chapter 16

Some Things to Help Along with the Manifestation Process

There are some tricks you can use to help along with the manifestation process. I'll list three effective ones here:

1. A vision board. You've probably seen or heard of this before. This is where you cut out a picture of your desire from a magazine and post it up on a board somewhere you can see all the time. It could be a picture of a car, house, dream vacation place, etc. By constantly focusing on this object you keep looking at, you attract it into your life.

   A vision board is a good thing, but you STILL have to follow the rules I talked about before. The best way to use a vision board would be to feel how you would if you already had your desire every time you walk by the board and glance at the picture. The key point is *GLANCE*. You have to glance at it very BRIEFLY and feel the emotion associated with it. Then you must put it out of your mind until you see it again sometime later. If you don't do this, and keep looking at the vision board and still think about your desire right after, your Conscious mind will stop your Subconscious mind from doing its work. You have to do it like the on/

off light-switch analogy I talked about earlier. You either briefly think about your desire with emotion, or you don't think about it at all. Do not allow thoughts of your desire to linger when you're not visualizing it. That's the secret to making a vision board work.

2. *Snagit software.* Snagit is computer software that allows you to instantly capture anything you see on your computer screen and save it as an editable picture file. Instead of having a physical vision board, you can use your computer screen as a vision board. During the day, you can open the picture file, glance at it, feel the emotion associated with it, close or minimize the picture, and completely forget about it until you open the picture again. Snagit allows you to modify the picture in any way.

You can do some real neat things with this feature. For example, you can take a screen shot of your bank account. If your balance is, say, $3,000, you can crop the balance out and put in $30,000. Then you would use this as your computer vision board every day. If you keep focusing on this picture in your mind every day, with emotion, some coincidence may come where you'll get $30,000. Or you may get an intuition on how to earn $30,000. Take action when you do. Snagit can be purchased online for download.

Don't get too carried away in the beginning. If you put in $300,000, your logical mind may not accept this as true right now and will fight your Subconscious mind. Remember, the key is to get your Conscious and Subconscious minds in agreement for things to work. That is why sustaining your belief is also very important.

3. *Audio products.* You may have come across such products as brain entrainment music for manifestation and the like. These aren't bad things; you just have to keep in mind that no matter what you get, you'll be fine as long as you still go by all the rules I outlined in detail throughout this book.

Chapter 17

Things That Are Very Difficult or Impossible to Manifest

Now I know this chapter is going to sound like heresy, because no other book on the law of attraction talks about what you CANNOT do. They all teach you that anything is possible and if you dream it, you can do it. I fully agree that the law of attraction and our powers of manifestation can do amazing, great, and incredible things for us. However, there still are certain situations where things are difficult, even impossible, to manifest, so it's not worth the time and energy to try to visualize them.

First, you have to understand that every single person has the ability to manifest. When masses of people are thinking a certain way and you're trying to think another, your one Subconscious mind simply cannot overpower one million or more Subconscious minds that are working against you.

Here are a few unusual examples to illustrate some of those impossible situations. I'm sure you'll get the idea and can think of a few after reading these:

1. Trying to be president of the United States and not being a citizen at birth. It would be pointless for people to visualize

themselves as president of the United States when they don't meet any of the various criteria, such as being a natural-born citizen. Unless a HUGE mass of people visualize and take action toward changing this rule, it'll never happen for the one person who visualizes becoming president. Throughout history, things that were thought to be impossible were accomplished but were done so with the support of large masses of people. When you combine the belief and Subconscious power of a large mass of people, then you can change difficult or seemingly impossible situations. The American Revolution is a good example of this.

2. Winning the lottery or a sweepstakes. Now, I'm not saying it's impossible to win a large amount of money by the law of attraction. It's very possible. However, realize that there are thousands of other people who think and feel the exact same way you do during every drawing. So, while it's not impossible to win big jackpots with the law of attraction, it's not easy either. The things you have the best chance at manifesting are things that pertain to your OWN particular circumstances.

3. Playing in professional sports. This category is difficult, but not impossible to manifest. While there are many who play professional sports, the vast majority of us never get a chance. Some things are just God-given talents that people are born with. I love to play basketball and would love to play professionally in the NBA. But no matter how much I visualize it, it's not likely to ever happen. I would NOT discourage someone with high potential to dream that one day he/she can play professional sports. But for the vast majority, we still have to be somewhat realistic and not expend our mind energy on things that have a very low chance of happening.

4. When it's a bad economy. When the country is in a deep recession and your business is down, you should use your knowledge of the law of attraction to increase your business despite the circumstances. However, most people don't understand the law of attraction and follow the media closely. The media uses the element of FEAR to keep the masses interested in their stories. Have you noticed most news reported is NEGATIVE? When people are scared, they are afraid to take action. In a recession, people are fearful, uncertain, and afraid to spend money. Since the VAST majority of people FEEL negative and afraid in their Subconscious minds, it will be a more difficult task to attract business with the law of attraction during a recession than when the economy is good. If the majority of people apply the law of attraction and keep their focus on feeling good and abundant despite the recession, the situation can improve much faster.

The bottom line is, if the masses of the people are against you in general (or if everyone is going for one prize), it is difficult to manifest something unless the masses completely change their way of thinking.

I can still give more examples of difficult to impossible situations, but I'm sure you get the idea. Use your common sense and a sense of being realistic to determine what you want. Don't ever forget, there ARE a GREAT number of things you CAN accomplish with your mind and the law of attraction and manifestation. The key is to know what it is exactly that you want first and then apply the proper techniques to obtain it.

Chapter 18

~

Some Other Key Points to Keep in Mind

I'd like to spend some time here to discuss a few other key points that typically aren't covered in other books.

Don't expend energy trying to change other people with what you have learned. If other people are very willing to learn about the law of attraction, then by all means associate with them. You'll come to learn that when you help others get what they want, you'll eventually get what you want, though not necessarily from the person you helped. We've all heard the principle "For every action, there is an equal and opposite reaction." This law of physics applies just as much to the law of attraction, although there is a TIME DELAY so it's not as obvious.

However, if some people are not receptive to your energy, don't use your knowledge to try to force or change them. Remember detachment? Accept people for what they are and let go. Focus on changing YOURSELF. We can't change the world all at once. The only REAL way to change the world is to do it one person at a time, and that starts with OURSELVES.

I would like to go back to the chapter where I said that you must first decide CLEARLY what it is you want. When you ask people what it is they want exactly, you'll be surprised to see that most people won't be able to tell you what they want. If anything, they can give you a whole list of what they DO NOT want! If you're in this group, train yourself to keep your energy and focus only on things that you WANT. It sounds illogical, but people as a rule tend to focus on the negative (like the news) and what they don't want. If you understand the law of attraction, if you keep focusing on negatives, you can't possibly be solving any of your problems. You'll only attract MORE of the same negativity to you. As I have said many times, you should be AWARE of negative possibilities. But focus the majority of your thoughts and especially your emotion on the PRESENCE of what you want rather than on the absence of it.

There may be times where you really desire something but things don't work out the way you expected them to. It would seem on the surface that the law of attraction didn't work. Actually, the law of attraction is always working. But there's a key point I'd like to mention here. As you know, your Subconscious is connected with the Ether, or universal power. It knows things that your logical Conscious mind has no way of understanding. It could be that the thing you visualized and desired might not be right for you.

For example, say there's someone you want to be with and you visualized yourself married to that person. Unknown to you, maybe the marriage might not have worked out later on, so your Subconscious prevented that from happening.

Another situation along the same lines could be that you visualized yourself coming into a good opportunity. When that time arrived, you didn't get it or it didn't turn out the way you had expected. You have to understand that many times these failures are actually blessings in disguise by your Subconscious. It's highly likely your Subconscious has a BETTER opportunity waiting for you later on. You have to have faith that things will work out, be persistent, and be DETACHED to any seemingly negative things that may happen during the attraction process.

Being detached is ever so important. It has been said being detached is the state of enlightenment. When you are detached and

NOT attached to a certain expectation, you allow the infinite power of the universe to bring you your desire in ways you'd never expect.

There may be times when you're persistent with your visualizations, but nothing appears to be happening. Do not go by what you see. The creation and attraction process happens on the higher planes, which are not visible to your five senses. You have to continue to have faith, BELIEVE, PERSIST, and PERSEVERE. This will eventually lead to success.

A lot of times, when people start to learn about the law of attraction and manifesting, they get a little carried away and start to imagine things that are too large for themselves to handle at the moment. As a result, their logical Conscious mind is not able to believe that such a thing is possible. When that happens, they say the law of attraction doesn't work. The truth is, it does work. The situation you visualize and try to manifest should be greater, but NOT way too far from your current situation, at least in the beginning. Once you attain the new and better situation, you can GRADUALLY move up from there.

For example, if some people are currently making $30,000 a year, and they try to manifest $1,000,000 a year, it is not likely things will work in their favor. They should maybe go from $30,000 to $60,000 a year, and slowly move upward from there. If you're renting a small one-bedroom apartment and desire to own a million-dollar home, you should first visualize yourself owning a $150,000 home, and then move up gradually. Don't overwhelm yourself in the beginning and end up getting discouraged with the results.

How Continued Awareness Leads to Attachment

I'd like to return to the subject of awareness. Remember how I said you should only be aware, but NOT dwell on negative possibilities? Let's examine for a moment what actually happens when you start to be constantly aware of something based on everything we've learned in this book so far.

Think of something good or bad. We'll use bad as an example first. If you're constantly aware of something bad that can happen, you eventually start to ANTICIPATE that it will happen. When you constantly anticipate what will happen, that leads to ATTACHMENT, which, as explained before, is a negative emotion in the form of fear. In this case, you're afraid of something you don't want to happen. Going by the law of attraction, you attract more negative situations of fear to yourself. This is why people who are always paranoid of everything seem to consistently attract negative situations to themselves. They are constantly aware of or dwelling in their thoughts that some imaginary person or thing is out to get them.

Another type of person in this category is the one who is too overly cautious and goes overboard on taking precautions for everything. As I discussed in chapter 12, being aware or cautious of the negative prevents it from happening. But that means only a split-second awareness. When people are too overly cautious and become obsessed with taking precautions for everything, trying to prevent something, they usually end up experiencing the negative event they tried to avoid.

When people go to astrologers and get a negative reading, they get frightened and start becoming constantly aware of that negative possibility. So this constant awareness turns into anticipation. They start taking extreme precautions to prevent this from happening. But because they keep focusing on this, they will end up creating and getting the negative situation they tried so hard to avoid or prevent. The astrologer seemed to have amazing abilities but, in fact, it was the person who created it for themselves through the law of attraction! Genuine astrology is able to predict the way the future is SUPPOSED to be at a given moment. However, that future, if negative, can EASILY be changed by an individual if he/she stops dwelling on the negative and immediately changes their thoughts and corresponding actions. Astrologers know this, and the genuine ones should be able to guide their clients AWAY from the negative possibilities.

On the other hand, let's say you're constantly aware of something good, something you desire and visualized. If you're constantly aware of it, you start to anticipate that it will happen. When you constantly anticipate that it will happen, you have a tendency to develop an attachment to it. You start to think you can't live without it. Attachment is a form of fear. You're afraid you might not get what you want. Fear is the number-one enemy of the Subconscious mind. In the end, you don't get what you visualized. This attachment to something positive or negative always brings about a NEGATIVE result. Now allow me to reveal to you the great secret of secrets:

*The ultimate state of mind to be in is a CONSTANT STATE OF DETACHMENT and at the same time a positive attitude. Another way of saying this is: Learn to ACCEPT whatever negative things come into your life and feel happy within, no matter what your outer circumstances appear to be. When you do this, you're not letting outside things affect you to any major extent. You accept those things for what they are, and at the same time you're continuously attracting good things to yourself. That's the greatest secret of all.

Only 2 percent of your day should be spent visualizing what you want. The other 98 percent should be focused on finding reasons to FEEL happy, confident, and grateful for everything. Also, do your best to FORGET about what you want as well as the negative things in your life.

Chapter 19

In Conclusion

I have tried my best throughout this book to present the law of attraction and manifestation in the most basic and direct manner possible. I've included the theory behind everything I've explained, when necessary, but my emphasis in this book is on being able to use the PRACTICAL techniques I've discussed every day.

*The absolute MOST important thing to do when one acquires good practical information is to APPLY it. You can read all the books, go to all the seminars, but if you never APPLY anything you've learned, all the knowledge you have is useless. Knowledge alone is NOT power. APPLIED KNOWLEDGE IS POWER. Then you must practice your new skill to become proficient at it. Practice does NOT make perfect. PERFECT PRACTICE MAKES PERFECT!

Sometimes when you start to use the law of attraction and manifestation, people such as friends and family will tell you, "It doesn't work" and make other negative comments that will put doubt into your mind. The best thing to do is to keep everything to yourself and not tell anyone until you get what you desire. Then there can be no doubt as to whether or not it works.

There are going to be times when your own mind will work against you, creating doubt. Maybe you're living in an apartment, and you desire to live in a house. So you visualize, with emotion, a house you desire. A little imaginary voice might pop into your head that will say, "There's no way you can live in a house like that. That's beyond your means. Don't think about it."

That's normal; it is your logical Conscious mind trying to protect you by keeping you in your comfort zone. You have to train yourself to get past that and persist in your efforts. Eventually, your Conscious mind will start to believe it too, and once your Conscious and Subconscious are working together, great things start to happen.

You'll see a lot of courses and books that support using affirmations to attract your desires. Affirmations are positive statements that, when repeated over and over, are supposed to attract your desire to you. Reciting affirmations is a good thing to do, but the most important thing is to monitor your state of emotions and make sure you stay positive. One powerful manifestation session and being detached will be more effective than saying an affirmation over and over again without any emotion.

Everything you've experienced in your life has been from habitual thoughts passed from your Conscious mind into your Subconscious mind and activated through BELIEF in those thoughts. Now that you know this, stop thinking to yourself "I can't do it," "I can't afford it," "There's no way," "I don't have any money," etc. All these negative, persistent thoughts make their way into your Subconscious mind and produce more of the same negativity in your life. Instead, even though your circumstance may not be good right now, turn those thoughts around. If you pass by an item in the mall you'd like to have, think and feel to yourself, "I can afford it." Always think, feel, and believe "I have money," and "All things are possible through my Subconscious mind." When you make a habit of putting these kinds of positive thoughts into your Subconscious mind, it will respond by gradually bringing you positive situations (to give you what you want) instead of negative ones.

⁓

*Engage in activities that make you FEEL GOOD and excited. Keep your thoughts and emotions toward the positive things in life. Avoid people who are constantly negative about their life and the world. This will keep you in a high emotional/vibrational state and you'll make it a habit of attracting good circumstances toward yourself.

⁓

*To manifest back the cost of this book, apply everything you have learned. Visualize with emotion an image of yourself holding a check in the amount of the cost of this book. That's all you need to do. Don't bother with how it's going to happen. Just clearly picture only that image. Believe it to be true. Do this every single day for thirty days. Your Subconscious mind has immense power. If you visualize this without fail for a month, you should easily manifest back the relatively small cost of this book. After you succeed with this, you can start manifesting with confidence your other TRUE heart's desires! Try to manifest one thing at time. If you focus too much mind energy on too many different things all at once and not enough on ONE thing, you may not get the results you want.

Take note: a big project you wish to manifest will require MORE mental energy and TIME to show up in your circumstances versus a smaller project.

In closing, there is one very important principle to keep in mind. You can wish for or desire anything. However, you also have to accept everything that comes along with it. For instance, if you want to live in a million-dollar home, you have to accept that there will be high property taxes and extensive maintenance costs that go along with it. If you want an expensive luxury car, you have to accept that there will be high costs associated with maintaining and servicing the vehicle. If you want a higher-paying job, you have to accept that there will be many more responsibilities required once you get that job.

We've all heard that we can't get something for nothing, which is true. If you want something, you have to first expend mind energy to manifest it to reality. Once you have it, you have to accept the responsibilities that come along with it. If you understand that, then the circumstances in your life can only get better and better.

Success = Patience + Persistence + Perseverance

Faithfully apply the secrets you have learned and you are certain to see amazing results!

A More Detailed Explanation of the Law of Attraction and Quantum Physics

I didn't want to get into too much theory in the beginning because I promised that I would keep things as practical as possible. Now that you have a solid working knowledge of the law of attraction, I reserved this bonus chapter to explain in much greater detail (for those scientific people out there) just HOW quantum physics really proves that everything I've revealed in this book about the law of attraction is absolutely true.

In 1925, the great Albert Einstein (*Time* magazine's Person of the Century!) came to the amazing conclusion that everything is ultimately made up of the SAME ENERGY. This includes everything we can see and all things we cannot see, such as radio waves, X-rays, and even our THOUGHTS. As I discussed in chapter 2, Einstein formulated this everything-is-same-energy theory into the very famous equation $E = MC^2$. No one disputed Einstein's findings. However, the question that remained at that time was, if everything is ultimately energy, what *FORM* does it exist in—particles or waves? Einstein was certain that energy existed as particles. But another famous scientist at that time named Thomas Young was certain that energy existed as waves. The debates went back and forth on this.

Well, along came a brilliant Nobel Prize–winning physicist named Niels Bohr who speculated that energy could exist as BOTH particles and waves. As technology really advanced, machines called particle accelerators allowed scientists to determine that energy starts out as a wave of probability. When conscious awareness is placed on a wave, the wave of probability "collapses" and turns into a definite particle. Does that make sense? Let me explain it this way. The wave of probability can be anything you want it to be. You want a new car, a house, a vacation, or a new job. Let's say for now you want a new car. The wave has no form yet. When you start to think about the car with emotion, you're putting your AWARENESS on the wave. The wave now collapses into a tiny particle of a car from your thought of a car. All other probabilities collapse, or are gone, because the tiny particle can only now be a car. It can't possibly be anything else!

Try to picture me holding a string from end to end. That's a wave that could potentially be anything we want it to be. Now picture me rolling the string into a little ball with my fingers. That's the wave collapsing into a definite particle as a result of a person's thought or awareness on it.

Here's the REALLY amazing part: If a scientist who was studying this energy expected or believed to see particles, then particles would be seen. If the scientist expected or believed to see waves, then waves would be seen. So, the energy that the scientists were studying would turn into either particles or waves depending on the belief of the scientist! Doesn't that blow your mind?

Do you recall in chapter 1 when I said it all starts with your beliefs? Let's use what we learned in this chapter and put it together with what we learned before in chapter 5.

Whatever it is you think about, you impress into the invisible Ether of space, which is full of waves. This thought or awareness changes a probability wave into a definite particle. In other words, a human thought causes a wave in space to collapse into a particle. And just like the scientists experienced, the particle turns into something based on what you believe in. If you believe you're visualizing a car, the particle eventually becomes a car. If someone else believes it's a house, it eventually becomes a house. Your belief controls the whole process and completely determines the results. And, of course, if you don't believe it will happen, it won't! That's why believing really does make all the difference in the world, literally and scientifically!

Now let me get into something truly astonishing. These particles of energy that started out as waves are "intelligent." They have the ability to communicate with one another at any moment. Time and space are not issues. So what does that mean? It means that when you visualize something, you first convert a wave in space into a particle. The more you visualize it, the more particles there are. These particles can attract each other through communication, and since time and space aren't problems, these particles can attract more of each other at a moment's notice. It doesn't matter how far apart they are! That's why, according to the law of attraction, like attracts like. These particles you created from your thought can communicate and will attract more of one another through the law of attraction.

Over time, all the particles get large enough physically and show up in your reality through coincidences or intuition! Since everything is ultimately energy and things attract each other according to how fast they vibrate, you'll sometimes see the law of attraction being called by another name, the law of vibration. They both mean the same thing.

Here is an important concept I leave you with in this chapter. Since everything is energy, WE ARE ALL ONE and the same energy. We are all connected as one BIG system. When we help one person in this world move forward, we help the whole system. Good things will come to you when you help someone get what they want, though not necessarily from the person you helped. The reverse is also true. If someone hurts another person, negative things will happen to them, and not necessarily from the person they hurt. Never use the law of attraction to hurt others!

Besides making the effort to feel as positive all the time as much as you can, try to help others get what they want if you have the opportunity to do so. When you do that, you're constantly attracting good situations to yourself and even greater things to the world by contributing to the whole system of energy.

—

Always Watch Your State of Emotions

This chapter goes more into detail from what you first learned in chapter 2. Recall that your feelings are the most important factor in determining what you attract into your life. Therefore, the constant monitoring of your state of emotions is perhaps the single most important thing when it comes to daily use of the law of attraction. Other books on the law of attraction and positive thinking usually teach that "thoughts become things." That's NOT quite the whole picture. If I didn't make this clear before in chapter 2, let me make it very clear here: Thoughts do NOT necessarily become things. It is the EMOTIONS associated with thoughts that make them become things.

The law of attraction as we know it covers two main aspects of our lives. The first is what we're attracting to ourselves all the time, every minute of the day. The second is using it systematically (as I've taught throughout this book) to bring a specific person, thing, or circumstance to us at will.

In both of these situations, emotions play the major role. When you're visualizing your desire, you need to use emotion as the fuel to bring your thought to reality. When you're not visualizing your desire, which is most of the time, you need to watch your state of emotions.

Remember from chapter 3 how your Subconscious mind is responsible for shaping your outer circumstances? It does this entirely through your EMOTIONS. Think of your Conscious mind as a farmer and your Subconscious mind as a large field of rich soil. All thoughts from the Conscious mind (farmer) are SEEDS that get PLANTED into your Subconscious mind (the soil). When EMOTION is attached to those seeds of thought, it creates the perfect environment where those seeds can grow into crops, or I should say, CIRCUMSTANCES.

This is why you should always find reasons to FEEL good and positive. This will cause your Subconscious mind to continuously attract good situations to you. At times there will be certain situations that are out of your control, that will cause you to experience negative feelings. But you should make every effort to monitor your state of emotions to keep them positive the majority of the time. I don't like to mention negative emotions, but one negative emotion you should definitely try to train yourself to avoid is anger. Not only is it bad for you physically, but this intense emotion can only attract more negative circumstances to yourself. Is it mere coincidence that the word "anger" is just one letter short of the word "danger"?

Your Subconscious mind never sleeps. It is awake twenty-four hours a day, seven days a week. It controls all the involuntary functions of your body, such as your heartbeat, breathing, digestion, and the like. At the same time, it constantly attracts (and creates) good or bad circumstances to you based on your positive or negative emotions associated with your thoughts.

Next time you go to the mall or a department store, make the effort *not* to think thoughts like "I can't afford this" or "That's too expensive." Train yourself to think you *can* afford anything and give yourself the feeling you can even though you can't at the present moment. Start gradually planting consistent SEEDS of "I can" into your Subconscious mind with your positive emotion. (Remember, the Subconscious mind is affected by emotion and REPETITION.) Also, think to yourself that even though you can afford something, you don't necessarily have to possess it in order to be happy. This does two really important things for you. First, it gives you a feeling of abundance, which will graduall y bring you more circumstances of abundance. And second, it trains you to be DETACHED from your desires. And you already know from chapter 9 how extremely important it is to be detached for things to work out.

Once in a while, do buy something of good quality for yourself that you've been wanting. By doing so, you give yourself the FEEL-ING that you're worth it and you will attract more circumstances of abundance to yourself. Don't interpret this as going on a massive shopping spree. You still have to use common sense and manage your finances. But buying something of value for yourself from time to time that makes you feel good emotionally is important to keeping more good things coming to you. Keep your daily focus and feeling on abundance of wealth (even though you may not have much now) instead of lack, and you'll gradually attract more wealth.

Although this book is not a specialized instructional course on how to make money, the very first step to being wealthy/abundant is the feeling of being wealthy/abundant. Motivational speakers refer to this as the wealth mind-set. This also includes the way we look at other people. We typically feel envious when we see people with more wealth or luxury than ourselves. However, if you want to make the law of attraction work for you, you have to start training yourself to think and feel that the universe is all abundant, despite what your situation seems like at the moment. There is more than enough for everyone. Instead of being envious, be happy for those people who have wealth and luxury. Realize that, in time, you too can achieve wealth when you apply the law of attraction by changing your habit-ual state of thoughts and emotions.

Again, thoughts by themselves do NOT necessarily become things. It's the EMOTIONS associated with thoughts that produce the results. A thought without emotion is like a car without any gas-oline. It's not going to go anywhere. You can think of emotion as gasoline. Gasoline provides the energy needed to move the car and, by the same analogy, emotion is the energy needed to bring thought into physical reality.

Let me take this one step further. The gasoline isn't enough to move the car. You still need a spark to ignite the gasoline. Well, the spark needed to ignite the emotion to manifest the thought is belief. I know I talked a lot about belief in the previous chapters, but let me briefly review it here. Sustained belief in the Conscious mind that the thought is true ignites the emotion to bring the thought to reality.

"Belief" is a more modern word for "faith." But did you realize that "PERSISTENCE" is also another word for faith? Let's say you visualize something you want and that little voice in your head tells you it's not possible. Maybe you have a hard time believing it to be possible. That's human nature, and it's normal. But remember, the Subconscious mind responds to EMOTION and REPETITION. If you persist with your visualizations day after day, that basically means you have faith. If you didn't have faith or belief, you wouldn't persist, would you? So realize that every little seed or thought you habitually plant every day into your Subconscious mind through EMOTION and BELIEF will show up in your circumstances over time. Since we're planting seeds all the time, we might as well be planting seeds of confidence, abundance, wealth, and happiness!

I leave you with a very important principle in this chapter. And that is, YOUR OUTER WORLD IS A GRADUAL REFLECTION OF YOUR INNER WORLD. You may not be completely aware of it, but what you see in your present circumstances is a direct reflection of your PAST inner thoughts and emotions. When you look into a mirror, your reflection in the mirror is your outer circumstances. YOU are the inner thoughts and emotion. Too often, when people don't understand the law of attraction, they go about trying hard to change their outer circumstance without changing the way they think and feel toward the circumstance. But that's like changing an undesirable reflection in the mirror by simply changing the mirror. That's not getting to the source of the problem. You have to change the source of the reflection in the mirror.

By the same analogy, to change a current undesirable circumstance, you need to start by changing the way you think and feel toward it. Do understand that when you make the decision to start thinking and feeling positive all the time, visible changes won't appear overnight. But over time, your outer circumstances will slowly change to match your inner thoughts and emotions. Always keep in mind the time delay factor when it comes to the law of attraction.

It has always been a dream of mine to reveal the most powerful secrets on the law of attraction and to explain it in a manner anyone can understand. I've studied most of the older books on the subject as well as a lot of the newer books. Please feel free to contact me if you feel something is missing or needs to be addressed. Now that you know the secrets to getting what you want, I wish you the absolute best of success with using the law of attraction!

About the Author

David Che is a practicing general dentist in Cocoa Beach. He received his Doctor of Dental Surgery degree in 2001 from the University of Illinois at Chicago. The subject of the law of attraction and manifestation has fascinated him since he was a child. He lives in Florida.